The Man Who Loved Again

Ivan Lloyd Roquero

Published by Ivan Lloyd Roquero, 2024.

THE MAN WHO LOVED AGAIN

First edition. December 7, 2024.

ISBN: 979-8230078951

Written by Ivan Lloyd Roquero.

Also by Ivan Lloyd Roquero

Algorithmic Uprising
From Ground Zero to Fortune
The Man Who Loved Again

Table of Contents

The Man Who Loved Again

By Ivan Lloyd Roquero

"The greatest love story is not the one that never has problems, but the one that keeps fighting to overcome them."

Dedication:

To those who have loved, lost, and learned from their past, this story is for you. May you find strength in the struggles and hope in the healing. To my family and friends who supported me during the toughest moments of my life, your unwavering belief in me kept me going. This is for the ones who never gave up on love, even when it felt impossible.

Acknowledgements:

I would like to express my sincere gratitude to everyone who has been part of this journey, whether directly or indirectly. This story and the experiences shared would not have been the same without the support and encouragement of several individuals.

To my family and friends, thank you for your constant support and understanding. Your presence in my life has been invaluable, providing strength and comfort during the toughest moments And the lessons learned from you have been instrumental in shaping the person I am today.

I also want to acknowledge the moments of struggle, reflection, and personal growth that have been crucial to my development. These challenges, though difficult, have been my greatest teachers, helping me build resilience and perspective.

Lastly, I would like to thank myself for persevering through the hard times, for recognizing my own weaknesses, and for striving to become a better version of myself. It's through these experiences that I have learned the importance of self-awareness, patience, and growth.

This journey is ongoing, and I am deeply grateful for all the people and lessons that have contributed to it. Your support, whether seen or unseen, has made all the difference.

Hook:

Life has a way of testing our limits, pushing us to the edge, and forcing us to confront the darkest corners of our hearts. It's easy to get lost in the chaos of misunderstandings, trust issues, and broken connections, but somewhere within that struggle lies the potential for our growth and unexpected encounters. This is a story of love, pain, and the relentless pursuit of something real and something that even distance and time can't erase. The journey may not have been easy, but it's a testament to the power of second chances and the lessons we learn along the way.

Preface:

This story is not just a collection of events or a recount of past experiences. It's a reflection of my journey, the struggles, the mistakes, the growth, and everything in between. As I write these words, I realize how much time has passed, how much has changed, and how much I've learned from the people and moments that shaped my life.

The events within these pages are personal, some even painful to revisit. Yet, it's through sharing these vulnerable moments that I hope to offer something valuable not just for myself, but for anyone who may read this and find a part of their own story reflected here. This isn't a tale of perfection, but rather a testament to perseverance and learning through hardship.

Throughout my life, I've encountered people who have touched my heart in ways that I never expected. Some have stayed, some have left, and some remain only as distant memories. Each of them has played a role in shaping who I am today, and for that, I am thankful. In the process, I've discovered that love, friendship, trust, and heartbreak are all intertwined in a way that we can't control or predict. They unfold on their own, whether we're ready for them or not.

As you read this, I ask that you not only see the story but also understand the journey behind it the fears, the growth, and the moments of clarity that followed confusion. This story is an exploration of love, loss, and self-discovery, and I hope that through my words, you can find something that resonates with your own experiences.

This is more than just a story. It's a piece of me that I am offering to you honest, raw, and real. I hope it gives you something to hold onto, just as I've held onto the lessons learned along the way. Thank you for joining me on this journey, and I hope that you, too, can find strength in the midst of struggle, clarity after chaos, and peace after the storm.

Chapter 1: First Crush, First Lessons

I'd like to share my experiences related to love, as this is my first non-fiction book about those moments. I recently published my book titled "From Ground Zero to Fortune."

It all began when I was in the third grade and she was in the fifth. Although she was older than me, I thought, "Age doesn't matter." I saw her almost daily at school, but at that time, I didn't have any feelings for her, nor did I know her name.

After a few weeks, I asked a friend if he knew her name, and he told me it was "Lisa." A rush of happiness filled me when I learned it. One day, as I was heading to the canteen, I encountered her. Our eyes met, and nervously, I approached her with a smile and said, "Hi." I was afraid she might reject me, but to my delight, she responded with a cheerful "Hello" before continuing on her way to the canteen.

Once I got to my classroom, I opened Facebook to search for her profile. I found her and sent her a friend request, hoping she would accept. An hour later, I received a notification that she had accepted my request. Excited, I sent her a message, and to my relief, she replied. That was how our conversations on Facebook began.

Unfortunately, after a few weeks, Lisa became distant online. I had no idea why, so I stopped messaging her, though my feelings for her remained strong. One day, as I was walking home from school, I turned to my cousin Ann and said, "I want to ask you something about Lisa." She looked curious and replied, "What is it?"

Feeling shy, I continued, "Does Lisa have a crush on anyone?" Ann asked, "Why are you asking about that?" My nerves got the better of me, and I confessed, "I have a crush on her." Her reaction surprised me as she exclaimed, "Really?" I nodded and said, "Yes, I want to tell her how I feel, but I'm too shy. Can you tell her that I like her instead?" She smiled and replied, "Of course, I'll tell her tomorrow when I go to school."

The next day, my cousin confidently told Lisa about my crush on her. As I sat in class, I eagerly contemplated how Lisa might react. I wondered what her response would be and felt ready to face whatever came next, even if it meant she might not feel the same way.

Months passed since my cousin Ann told Lisa about my feelings. In my young and hopeful mind, I imagined so many possibilities. Would she smile at me in the hallway? Would she talk to me more during recess? But the reality was different.

Lisa started to act differently around me. At school, she avoided eye contact and kept her distance. The shy glances she used to give me turned into quick, deliberate looks away. Each time our paths crossed, I felt a mix of hope and anxiety, only to be met with silence.

I tried to act normal, but my thoughts wouldn't leave me alone. Was she uncomfortable because of what Ann told her? Did I ruin whatever connection we might have had? These questions came in my mind, louder each day.

One afternoon, I decided to asked in my cousin Ann again. "Do you think Lisa hates me?" I asked her nervously.

Ann gave me a reassuring smile. "No, she doesn't hate you. Maybe she's just shy. Or she doesn't know how to respond."

"Then why does she avoid me?" I asked, frustration creeping into my voice.

Ann paused for a moment before replying, "It's hard to say. Sometimes, even if someone likes you, they don't know how to show it. Maybe she's scared or confused."

That thought gave me a sliver of hope, but I knew I couldn't dwell on it forever.

The days turned into weeks, and my feelings for Lisa began to shift. I still admired her from afar, but the spark I once felt started to fade. It wasn't because she had changed or done anything wrong, but because I realized I couldn't keep holding onto something that wasn't meant to be.

One day, I saw her laughing with her friends near the canteen. She looked genuinely happy, and for the first time in weeks, I smiled too. Maybe it was better this way, her living her life and me learning to let go.

I told in my best friend John about the whole situation. "I think it's time for me to move on," I told him during lunch.

John nodded, a knowing look in his eyes. "It's for the best. There are so many girls out there, Ivan. Don't let one experience hold you back."

"But she was my first crush," I said, feeling of sadness. "I'll always remember her, even if it didn't work out."

"And that's okay," John replied. "First crushes teach you a lot. They make you stronger for the next one."

Looking back, my feelings for Lisa weren't just about her. They were about the excitement of discovering what it meant to like someone, the nervousness of confessing, and the bittersweet lesson of moving on. It was my first crush with love, and though it didn't turn out the way I'd hoped, it shaped the way I saw relationships from then on.

As the school year ended, I saw less and less of Lisa. By the time summer arrived, my feelings had become a distant memory. I had learned my first lesson about love: "sometimes, it's not about the outcome but about the courage it takes to put yourself out there."

As summer drew near, I found myself reflecting on how much I'd grown over the past year. Lisa was still at the edge of my thoughts, but not in the same way as before. It was no longer about what could have been; instead, it was about what I had learned.

One day, I stumbled upon my cousin Ann at home. She had her textbooks scattered across the dining table as she worked on a project.

Taking a seat across from her, I asked, "Do you think I should've done something differently with Lisa?"

Ann looked up from her work, her face softening. "Ivan, you did everything right. You expressed your feelings honestly. That takes courage. It's not about what you could've done differently—it's about understanding that not everyone will feel the same way, and that's okay."

Her words stayed with me. Maybe I was too young to fully grasp them at the time, but they sparked a new perspective. Instead of seeing the experience as a failure, I started viewing it as a stepping stone.

When the final day of school arrived, there was a buzz of excitement in the air. Students ran through the hallways, signing yearbooks and taking group pictures. I hadn't planned to talk to Lisa, but fate had other ideas.

As I walked toward the classroom to gather my things, I saw her standing near the lockers with her friends. My heart raced. A part of me wanted to keep walking, but another part knew this was my chance to end things on a good note.

Taking a deep breath, I approached her. "Hey, Lisa."

She looked surprised but smiled politely. "Hi, Ivan."

There was an awkward pause, and for a moment, I regretted coming over. But then I mustered the courage to say, "I just wanted to thank you. For everything. I know things were... awkward, but I really appreciated getting to know you, even if it was from afar."

Her expression softened, and she nodded. "Thanks, Ivan. That's really sweet of you to say."

I could tell she was sincere, and that small moment of kindness was all I needed. As I walked away, I felt a weight lift off my shoulders. It wasn't closure in the traditional sense, but it was enough for me to move forward.

That summer, I threw myself into new activities to distract myself. I joined swimming, started reading adventure novels, and even learning to fight—something I'd always wanted to try. Each new interest became a reminder that life was full of possibilities, even beyond the world of crushes and unrequited love.

One afternoon, while swimming with my friends in Villa Garcia, I found myself laughing and shouting when we train for swimming. For the first time in months, I wasn't thinking about Lisa. I was fully present, enjoying the moment for what it was.

Later that evening, as the sun dipped below the horizon and the sky turned shades of orange and pink, I sat on the swings in the outside, reflecting on how much I'd changed. Lisa had been my first crush, my first lesson, and my first step into understanding what love could be. But she wasn't the end of my story, she was just the beginning.

By the time the new school year rolled around, I felt like a different person. I wasn't the shy, nervous boy who struggled to express his feelings anymore. I was more confident, more self-assured. And though I hadn't forgotten Lisa, I was ready to embrace whatever the future held.

Walking into the schoolyard on the first day, I caught a glimpse of her talking to her friends. She looked happy, and I felt a sense of peace. Smiling to myself, I thought, Thank you, Lisa for teaching me how to love and let go.

As the school year progressed, I started to understand the deeper lessons that came with my first crush. It wasn't just about the initial infatuation, or the excitement that surged when I saw Lisa in the hallway. The true lesson lay in the quiet moments of self-reflection, the understanding that feelings aren't always reciprocated, and how to navigate the emotional terrain when they aren't.

I spent a lot of time with my friends that year, particularly John, who had become a voice of reason whenever my thoughts drifted back to Lisa. He noticed the change in me, how I wasn't as obsessed with the idea of her anymore. He was right. I had started to focus more on myself, on the things I wanted to achieve. The more I grew, the clearer it became that I needed to learn to love myself before anyone else.

One afternoon, during a lunch break, John pulled me aside. "You've changed, man," he said with a grin, as he nudged me in the shoulder. "In a good way."

I smiled, taking a bite of my sandwich. "I guess you could say I'm starting to understand that not everything is about her anymore."

John nodded, his expression turning serious. "That's good. You shouldn't let one person define your happiness. You've got to find that for yourself. It's your life, Ivan."

His words resonated with me. They weren't just about Lisa they were about life in general. The idea of finding my own happiness, independent of anyone else's actions or feelings, was something I hadn't fully grasped before.

It was also around this time that I started paying more attention to my own growth. and I started taking my studies more seriously. I wasn't just going through the motions anymore. I set small goals for myself, aiming to improve in different areas. Each success, no matter how small, made me feel like I was becoming a better version of myself. The more I focused on my own development, the more the past seemed like a distant memory.

But the moment I knew I had fully moved on from Lisa was when I encountered her again. It had been several months since we last spoke, and I had changed so much since then.

It was during a school assembly, and I was walking through the hallway when I saw her standing near the lockers. This time, though, I didn't feel that familiar flutter in my chest. Instead, I felt calm. I gave her a polite nod and smiled, and she smiled back. We exchanged a few words about the assembly, but it was nothing more than a casual conversation. There was no lingering nervousness, no unease. Just two people who had shared a moment in time and had moved forward.

That was the moment I realized I had learned the most important lesson: life moves forward, whether you want it to or not. You can't stop time, and you can't hold onto the past forever. Eventually, you have to let go and make room for new experiences.

After that, the days continued to pass, and the more I immersed myself in new experiences, the clearer it became that the journey wasn't about finding love, it was about learning to love life, and myself. I began to understand that love wasn't just about grand gestures or feelings of infatuation. It was about growth, patience, and accepting that things don't always go as planned.

One evening, as I sat at the park alone, looking up at the stars, I couldn't help but feel grateful. Grateful for the lessons I had learned, for the pain I had experienced, and for the clarity that had come from all of it. I had learned that it was okay to feel hurt, but it was also okay to let go.

As I walked home that evening, I knew my journey had just begun. I didn't know what the future held, but I was ready to face whatever came next, knowing that the most important thing was to keep moving forward.

That's when I realized how everything was connected, the way Lisa had been my first crush, but also my first lesson in love and loss. How the experiences we have, even the ones that seem insignificant at the time, shape who we become. I had learned that to truly love someone, you had to first understand what it meant to love yourself and to embrace your own growth.

And so, my first crush became more thanjust a fleeting moment in time. It was a chapter in my life that had taught me something invaluable: that love, in all its forms, begins with self-love and the willingness to learn, grow, and move on when necessary.

I was no longer the shy, anxious kid I once was. I was starting to build my own identity, one that didn't rely on the approval of others. I didn't need to have a crush to feel validated. I didn't need to win anyone's affection to feel complete. I had everything I needed within myself.

As I walked through the halls of school, looking at the faces of my classmates, I understood that love wasn't about perfection it was about embracing the messiness of life. It was about making mistakes and learning from them. It was about understanding that life is not a fairy tale, and not every story has a happy ending, but that doesn't make it any less valuable.

In the end, Lisa wasn't the love of my life. But she was the first lesson. And for that, I would always be grateful.

Chapter 2: A Summer to Remember: First Love Across Miles

It all started one summer in Cebu, when I was around the age of 12. I had been visiting the city with my family, staying for what seemed like an eternity almost seven months. But as much as I enjoyed being in Cebu, I didn't want to go back to Bohol. The thought of returning to school felt like a distant and unnecessary task. Instead, I found myself spending more and more time exploring the city, discovering new places, and making memories that would later define my understanding of love, friendship, and personal growth.

One afternoon, as I wandered near a small computer shop, I noticed a girl standing by the entrance. She had a certain glow about her a mix of confidence and curiosity that caught my eye. Something about her made me want to approach her. Maybe it was her smile, or the way she stood there so at ease with herself. I'd never seen her before, and I was desperate not to let this moment pass me by. I had to talk to her, even if it meant breaking through the shell of shyness I often hid behind.

I approached her hesitantly, pretending that I needed directions to the very computer shop she was standing by. I knew exactly where it was, but I didn't care. I just needed a reason to speak to her.

"Hey, do you know where the computer shop is? I'm kind of lost," I asked, trying my best to sound casual.

She gave me a polite smile and responded, "Oh, it's just right here! Come with me, I'm headed there anyway."

As we walked toward the shop, I felt an excitement bubbling in my chest. This was it, the moment I had to make count. I couldn't afford to regret letting this opportunity slip through my fingers, like I had in the past. It felt like I was taking a small step toward something new, something unknown, but full of potential.

As we walked together, she asked, "So, what brings you here? What do you want to do at the computer shop?"

"I want to play Crossfire," I replied quickly, not really thinking about my answer. "I'm not very good at it yet though."

"Oh, I play Crossfire too! Do you want to play with me?" she asked, a twinkle of amusement in her voice.

I couldn't believe my ears. Here I was, talking to this beautiful girl, and she was offering to play a game with me? My heart raced, and I tried not to show how excited I felt.

"Yeah, of course! I need someone to help me out. I'm not good at this game at all," I responded, my voice more enthusiastic than I intended.

She chuckled, and we kept walking. She looked at me with a mixture of curiosity and amusement, asking, "So, where are you from?"

I hesitated for a moment before answering. "I'm from Bohol, actually. I'm just here on vacation."

She stopped in her tracks and turned to face me. "Oh, that makes sense. I thought you looked familiar, but I hadn't seen you around here before. I'm Bea."

Her name sounded like music to my ears. Bea. It was simple, yet it carried a certain grace. It felt so natural to speak with her, like we had known each other for far longer than we actually had. I smiled, and we shook hands before continuing our walk to the computer shop.

As we approached the entrance, she pulled out her phone, and it rang. It was her mom calling. I listened as Bea answered the call, and it wasn't long before I realized something interesting. She wasn't just any ordinary girl; she was the owner of the computer shop.

"Bea, where are you?" her mom's voice came through the speaker.

"I'm at the computer shop, Mom. Don't worry, I'm fine," Bea responded, smiling at me as she ended the call.

I couldn't hide my surprise. "Wait, you own the computer shop?" I asked, trying not to sound too amazed.

She shrugged, a playful grin on her face. "Yeah, why?"

I smiled and replied, "Just curious. I didn't expect to meet the owner of the place I was planning to go to."

We both laughed, and it felt easy, as if we were already friends. Soon, we were inside the shop, and Bea led me to one of the computer stations. I was still trying to wrap my head around the fact that I was actually spending time with this girl—this beautiful, confident, and easygoing girl who seemed to be everything I had always hoped for in a friend.

We spent the next few hours playing Crossfire together. Bea was patient with me, teaching me the ropes of the game. I wasn't a natural at it, but with her help, I quickly improved. Every time I managed to get a kill, she would smile at me with that encouraging look, and I felt a surge of pride. It wasn't just about the game anymore; it was about the connection we were forming.

Between matches, we chatted casually. She told me about her experiences playing Crossfire, her tips and tricks, and how she had been playing for almost two years. "When I first started, I kept dying all the time," she confessed, her eyes sparkling with mischief. "It was so frustrating, but eventually, I got better."

I smiled. "Yeah, I can definitely relate to that. It's tough in the beginning."

We both laughed, and for a moment, it felt like time had slowed down. The world outside the computer shop didn't matter anymore. It was just me and Bea, sharing this small moment in time, and I couldn't help but feel like something special was happening. Maybe it was the way she laughed at my jokes or how she taught me without making me feel bad for being a beginner. Or maybe it was the way we just clicked, like two pieces of a puzzle that had been waiting to fit together.

Eventually, the evening came to an end. Bea's mom called her, and it was time for her to go home. "Ivan, I have to go now. My mom wants me to head home. It's getting late," she said, standing up from her chair.

I felt a small pang of disappointment. I didn't want our time together to end, but I knew I couldn't keep her from her responsibilities. "Okay, take care. Thanks for teaching me how to play Crossfire. I really enjoyed it," I said, offering her a smile.

"No problem," she replied with a grin. "We can play again tomorrow. But I can't on Monday, I'll have school then."

"Got it. See you tomorrow," I said, watching as she walked out of the shop.

As I sat back in my chair, I couldn't wipe the smile off my face. It was a small encounter, but it felt significant. Bea had quickly become someone I looked forward to seeing every day. And little did I know, this was only the beginning of something much deeper.

The next few days passed in a blur, filled with more afternoons spent at the computer shop. Every time I saw Bea, I felt a mix of excitement and nervousness, like something was building between us, but neither of us knew exactly what it was. We continued to play Crossfire together, and I slowly began to get better at the game, thanks to her tips. More than that, though, it was the moments in between the games the conversations, the shared laughter that made me realize just how much I was looking forward to seeing her every day.

As we spent more time together, I noticed the little things about her. The way her eyes lit up when she talked about her favorite games or her excitement when she scored a perfect shot in Crossfire. She had this natural ease about her that made me feel comfortable, like we could talk about anything, no matter how random the topic.

One afternoon, as we were taking a break from gaming, we ended up sitting outside the shop on a bench. The sun was starting to set, casting a warm glow over everything, and the quiet hum of the city was the perfect background for our conversation.

"So, what do you want to do when you grow up?" I asked, genuinely curious.

Bea looked up at the sky for a moment, as if contemplating the question. "I don't know yet. I've always wanted to be a businesswoman, I guess. Owning this shop has been fun, but I want to do more. Maybe something in the tech field or even something to help people."

I smiled, impressed by her ambition. "That's really cool. I don't know what I want to do yet either, but I think I want to travel the world someday."

She grinned at me, "Travel the world, huh? That sounds nice. You can take me with you when you do."

I chuckled, not expecting her to say that. "Yeah? I'll be sure to bring you along."

We both laughed, and for a moment, it felt like we were two people who understood each other perfectly. I had only known Bea for a short time, but it already felt like we had been friends for ages. We could talk about anything business, life, the future and it all felt so natural.

But then, as the days went by, I noticed something else. When I wasn't around, I missed her. It wasn't just the fun of playing Crossfire or the excitement of a new friendship it was something more. I found myself thinking about her even when we weren't together. What was it? Was I just having fun, or was this something deeper?

It wasn't long before I realized the truth. I had developed feelings for Bea. The thought made my heart race. I wasn't sure if she felt the same way, but I couldn't ignore how I felt. Every time we talked, every time she smiled at me, my heart skipped a beat. It was like this silent connection between us, something I hadn't experienced before. And the more time I spent with her, the more I began to understand what it meant to care for someone.

One day, after our usual gaming session, we sat in the park nearby, eating ice cream. The evening air was cool, and the park was quiet, with only the sound of distant conversations and the occasional car passing by.

"Ivan, do you ever think about the future?" Bea asked, her voice soft.

"Yeah, sometimes," I said, turning to look at her. "But mostly, I just try to live in the moment. It's easier that way."

She nodded, taking a bite of her ice cream. "I guess you're right. But, sometimes, I wonder if things will always be the same. If we'll stay the same, or if we'll change."

I thought about her words for a moment. "We'll change, of course. But some things... some things will always stay the same. Like how we'll always remember the good times, right?"

Bea smiled at that. "Yeah, you're probably right."

As we sat there, enjoying our ice cream and the peaceful evening, I couldn't help but feel like this was one of those moments I'd always remember. The simple conversations, the laughter, the connection it was all so easy, yet so meaningful. And deep down, I knew I was falling for her. Slowly, quietly, but surely.

The next day, as I walked with Bea toward the computer shop, I made up my mind. I had to tell her how I felt. I couldn't keep pretending like nothing was happening between us. The connection was undeniable, and if I didn't act on it, I might regret it later.

As we approached the shop, I turned to her and said, "Bea, I need to tell you something."

She looked at me, her expression curious. "What is it?"

I hesitated for a moment, unsure of how to put my feelings into words. But then, I just decided to be honest. "I think... I think I like you. A lot. And I don't know if you feel the same way, but I just wanted to tell you."

Bea stopped walking, looking at me with wide eyes. For a moment, I felt like I might have said the wrong thing, like maybe I had overstepped. But then, she smiled softly. "I like you too, Ivan."

The words were a relief, more than I could have ever imagined. My heart skipped a beat as I realized that she felt the same way. We didn't say much more after that, but the air between us felt lighter, filled with the unspoken understanding that we were both feeling the same thing.

As the days went by, we continued to hang out, play Crossfire, and share our thoughts about life, the future, and everything in between. But now, there was something more between us. It wasn't just friendship anymore. It was something deeper, something that felt like the beginning of something special.

I didn't know where this was going, or how long it would last, but for the first time, I felt like I was exactly where I was supposed to be. With Bea. And that was enough for now.

As the days went on, my connection with Bea deepened, and I couldn't shake the feeling that everything we were experiencing together was like something out of a movie. We were young, carefree, and our days were filled with the thrill of new love, even if we didn't quite understand what it all meant. Every moment spent with her felt like a small adventure, whether we were hanging out at the computer shop, walking around the park, or having deep, philosophical conversations about the world. It was like our bond was growing stronger with each passing day.

But as time went by, I also began to feel a sense of urgency. I had to leave soon. My time in Cebu was coming to an end, and I had to return to Bohol to continue my studies. The thought of being apart from Bea was something I hadn't fully processed until now. It hit me like a wave how much I would miss her, how much I had grown to care for her.

I didn't want to think about it, though. Every day that I had left, I tried to focus on making the most of it. I cherished every moment, every glance, every laugh. I knew things wouldn't stay the same, but I wanted to hold on to these memories for as long as I could.

One afternoon, as Bea and I sat together on the steps of the computer shop, the sun beginning to dip below the horizon, I turned to her with a serious expression.

"Bea," I started, my voice quiet. "When I go back to Bohol... will we still be able to talk? I mean... will we still be friends?"

She smiled at me, her eyes filled with understanding. "Of course, Ivan. We'll always be friends. And you can always visit me when you come back to Cebu. I'll be here."

Her words gave me a sense of comfort, but they also reminded me of the distance that would soon separate us. We wouldn't be able to hang out every day, wouldn't be able to just walk to the park or play games together whenever we felt like it. The thought made my heart ache a little, but I pushed it aside. I still had time with her, and that was what mattered now.

The days flew by, and before I knew it, it was time for me to leave Cebu and return to Bohol. I packed my things, said goodbye to my relatives, and made the trip back home, but my mind kept drifting to Bea. How would things be between us now? Could we really stay connected despite the distance? I wasn't sure, but I hoped we would.

Once I arrived in Bohol, I tried to settle back into my routine, but it wasn't easy. I missed Bea more than I expected. There were times when I would be sitting in class, and my mind would wander to her, to the conversations we had shared, to the moments we spent laughing together. It was hard to focus on school when I kept thinking about her I'm still in the fourth grade that time.

But one day when I was in seventh Grade, while I was still adjusting to my new routine in Bohol, I received a message from her on Facebook. My heart skipped a beat as I opened the message, reading her words with a smile on my face.

"Ivan, how are you? I miss you. I hope we can talk more often."

It was then that I realized, despite the distance, we still cared for each other. We still wanted to keep our connection alive, even though we were miles apart. We kept in touch through messages, chatting whenever we could. We even made plans to talk on the phone when we had time.

Bea told me about her new life in the USA, her school, and the new people she had met. I told her about my life in Bohol, how school was going, and how much I missed her. We would talk for hours, even though the time difference between us made it difficult. But we made it work because we both knew how much it meant to us.

Over time, our bond grew stronger. We became more than just friends. We became a couple, despite the miles that separated us. We would talk about the future, about the possibility of me visiting her in the USA or her coming back to Cebu. We dreamed about the day when we would no longer have to say goodbye when we parted ways. But those were just dreams, and reality was much more complicated.

After one year of being in a long-distance relationship, things started to change. Bea's mom, who had always been protective of her, expressed concerns about her having a boyfriend. Bea told me that her mom didn't approve of our relationship anymore. I could tell from her voice that she was torn, but she explained to me that it was something she couldn't control.

"Ivan," Bea said one day over the phone, her voice sounding distant. "My mom doesn't want me to have a boyfriend. She says I need to focus on school and my future. I'm sorry..."

My heart sank. I didn't know what to say at first. I had known that long-distance relationships were difficult, but I never expected it to end like this. Bea had always been so supportive of our relationship, and now she was telling me it had to end because of her mom's wishes. I understood that family came first, but it didn't make it any easier.

"Bea... I understand. I really do," I replied, trying to keep my voice steady. "You have to do what's best for you."

"I'm really sorry, Ivan," she said softly. "I hope we can still be friends, though. I'll always care about you."

I felt a lump form in my throat, but I managed to say, "I'll always care about you too."

We said our goodbyes, and I hung up the phone, feeling a sense of emptiness wash over me. The one-year relationship that had meant so much to me was now over, just like that. I didn't know what the future held, but I knew that I would always look back on those memories with a sense of fondness.

The days after Bea and I ended our relationship felt heavy. For the first time in a long while, I didn't know how to fill the silence that had crept into my life. I tried to focus on school, on the activities that used to occupy my time, but it was as if something was missing. It was hard not to think of her, especially when memories of our time together kept resurfacing at the most unexpected moments.

I spent hours replaying our conversations, laughing at the inside jokes we shared, and remembering how easy it was to talk to her about anything and everything. It felt like we understood each other in ways no one else did. But I knew, deep down, that I had to let go. Life had its own plans for us, and sometimes, those plans didn't align with what we wanted.

As the days turned into weeks, I tried my best to push the sadness aside and focus on the things that mattered. School was demanding, but I found that it helped me take my mind off things. I threw myself into my studies, determined to excel and prove to myself that I could handle whatever came my way. The first few months after the breakup were a blur. There were moments when I would catch myself thinking about Bea, wondering how she was doing, but I quickly redirected my thoughts. I couldn't afford to dwell on the past.

Despite all of this, there was a part of me that held onto the hope that we would somehow reconnect. Every time I received a message from her, my heart would race. We still kept in touch on social media, chatting occasionally, sharing updates about our lives. She would tell me about her experiences in the USA, the new things she was learning, and how different her life had become. It was clear that she had moved on, in a sense, but there was still a part of her that cared. And I couldn't help but feel the same way.

However, as much as I wanted to hold onto the idea of us being together, I also knew that we were growing in different directions. Bea was in the USA, building her life there, and I was in Bohol, surrounded by the people and experiences that were shaping me. The distance between us wasn't just physical; it had become emotional too. Our conversations started to become less frequent, and eventually, I realized that we had both moved on in our own ways.

One afternoon, I sat alone on the steps outside my house, looking out at the horizon. The sun was beginning to set, casting an orange glow over the landscape. I took a deep breath and let the silence wash over me. For the first time since the breakup, I felt a sense of peace. I had let go.

I thought about how much I had learned from my relationship with Bea. It wasn't just about the good times we shared, the fun and laughter; it was about the growth that came from it. I had learned about love, about how to give and take in a relationship, and about the importance of respecting each other's dreams and goals. Even though things hadn't worked out between us, I would always cherish the lessons I had learned.

I also realized that I was ready to move forward. I was no longer the same person I was when I first met Bea. I had changed, grown, and learned. And although it hurt to let go, I understood that it was a part of life. Relationships come and go, but the lessons they teach us stay with us forever.

As the weeks went by, I began to focus more on myself and my future. I threw myself into my studies, started making new friends, and even explored new hobbies. I found comfort in the things that once felt unfamiliar to me. The more I focused on improving myself, the more I realized that I was stronger than I had given myself credit for. The heartbreak that had seemed so unbearable at first now felt like a distant memory.

But that didn't mean I had forgotten about Bea. She would always have a special place in my heart, and I would always remember her as my first love. I still had hopes for the future, dreams of traveling the world, of achieving things I never thought possible. I knew that life would bring new opportunities, new relationships, and new experiences. And when the time came, I would be ready to embrace them.

I continued to live my life, one step at a time, knowing that the end of one chapter wasn't the end of the story. There was always more to come. The heartbreak, the lessons, the growth, it was all a part of the journey that would shape me into the person I was becoming.

And so, as I walked through the halls of school, as I sat down to study, as I spent time with my friends and family, I carried with me the lessons of that first love. I knew that someday, when I looked back on this chapter of my life, I would smile, knowing that it had been worth it. It had been messy, complicated, and heartbreaking, but it had also been beautiful. And in that beauty, I found the strength to move forward.

Chapter 3: A Quick Love, A Short Goodbye

It was a bright and sunny day when I first met Ana in Anda, Bohol, a town known for its pristine beaches and tranquil atmosphere. I had been spending the summer at a friend's house, and that day, I decided to go for a swim in the clear blue waters, hoping to escape the pressures of my daily life and just enjoy the simple pleasures of the world. The sound of the waves crashing against the shore and the warmth of the sun on my skin made me forget the complexities of everything else.

I wasn't expecting anything to happen on that day, but life has a way of surprising you, doesn't it?

As I was walking along the shore, the salt in the air invigorating me, I noticed a group of people gathered near the edge of the water. One girl in particular caught my eye. She was standing with her friends, laughing and joking, her long hair swaying gently in the breeze. She seemed so carefree, so full of life, and there was something about her that made me want to walk up to her and start a conversation.

What was it that drew me to her? It wasn't just her beauty, though that was certainly part of it. It was something deeper maybe it was the way her energy seemed to radiate from her. She had this vibe, a kind of warmth and openness that I found magnetic. I stood there for a moment, just watching her, unsure of what to do next. I was shy, and even though I had a feeling this could lead to something special, I didn't know how to bridge the gap.

But then, before I could talk myself out of it, I took a deep breath, walked up to her, and said, "Hey. Nice day, huh?"

She looked at me, a little surprised, but then gave me a warm smile that put me at ease. "Yeah, it is," she said, her voice friendly and easygoing. "Are you from around here?"

I smiled, feeling the nerves in my stomach begin to settle. "No, actually. I'm from Sierra Bullones. I'm just here on vacation for a little while."

"Oh, that's cool!" she said, her eyes lighting up with curiosity. "I'm Ana. I'm from Candijay."

me most was how easy it was to talk to Ana. It felt like we had an unspoken connection, one that didn't need a lot of words to be understood. Her laughter was contagious, and every moment spent with her seemed to be filled with an undeniable energy that I couldn't quite explain.

A couple of weeks later, I found myself visiting Candijay, a small town not too far from where I lived, to see Ana again. I was excited to see her, but a bit nervous as well. Our conversations had been effortless, but now I was going to be face-to-face with her, away from the familiar environment of the beach, and I wondered if things would feel as natural as they had when we first met.

When I arrived, I was greeted by Ana at the tennis court. She was standing there, waiting for me, and I couldn't help but feel a flutter in my chest. She was wearing a simple t-shirt and shorts, but she looked effortlessly beautiful. There was something about the way she smiled at me that made my heart race.

"Hi!" she called out, waving enthusiastically.

"Hey," I responded, a little shy, feeling the weight of the situation hit me. I was usually more confident, but something about Ana made me nervous, in the best way possible.

We sat down together, but I found myself unable to think of much to say. It was like all the usual conversations I'd had with friends were out of my head. I was just so focused on her that I couldn't help but fall into a quiet silence. Ana didn't seem to mind, though. She was patient, just sitting there beside me, occasionally offering a comment or asking a question to keep the conversation going.

At some point, the awkwardness melted away, and we started talking again, picking up from where we had left off. We joked, shared more about our lives, and just enjoyed each other's company. I couldn't believe how easy it was to be around her. We walked around the town, and I even showed her some of my favorite spots, including a small café that I liked to visit when I needed a quiet moment. She seemed to appreciate the simplicity of it all, and I liked that about her.

But as the day began to wind down, something I wasn't prepared for happened. Ana's family invited me to stay the night at their home, since it was getting late and I didn't have a bus to take back to Sierra Bullones. I was hesitant at first, but the thought of spending more time with her made me say yes. Ana's parents were kind and welcoming, and they treated me like I was already part of the family, which made me feel a little more at ease.

That night, as I lay in the spare room of Ana's house, I thought about everything that had happened. We had only known each other for a few weeks, but it already felt like we were in a relationship, even without officially saying it. I wasn't sure where this would lead, but I couldn't help but feel a sense of happiness and excitement that I hadn't felt in a long time.

The next morning, we woke up early and spent the day exploring more of Candijay. We walked around the town, visited some of its historical sites, and talked about everything and nothing. I felt so comfortable around Ana, and I was beginning to think that maybe, just maybe, this could turn into something more.

But as quickly as we had come together, things began to shift. Two days later, after spending an unforgettable time together, we broke up.

I wasn't sure what had happened. One minute, everything felt perfect, and the next, it was as if the ground had been pulled out from under me. It wasn't a dramatic breakup there were no shouting matches or heated arguments. Instead, it was more of a quiet, almost resigned decision.

Ana said she needed space, that things were moving too quickly, and that she wasn't sure if she was ready for a relationship. I tried to understand, but a part of me was confused. We had just spent such an amazing time together, and I thought everything was going well. But in the end, I respected her wishes and agreed that maybe it was best to take a step back.

She told me that it wasn't anything I had done wrong, but rather that she needed time to figure things out for herself. I wanted to argue, to say that we could work through things, but deep down, I knew that sometimes things just don't work out, no matter how much we want them to.

As I left Candijay, I felt a mix of emotions. On one hand, I was grateful for the time we had spent together. The moments we shared our walks, our laughter, our quiet conversations were precious to me, and I wouldn't trade them for anything. But on the other hand, I couldn't help but feel disappointed, hurt by the abrupt end to something that had felt so right.

It didn't make sense. We had connected so easily, and I had believed, even for just a moment, that maybe this could be the start of something real. But life has a way of throwing curveballs at us, and sometimes, we just have to accept things as they are, no matter how hard it may be.

I didn't hear from Ana after that. We didn't stay in touch, and the silence between us grew. There was no closure, no explanation, just the quiet realization that sometimes, relationships don't last. I tried to move on, focusing on my schoolwork, my friends, and my hobbies, but the memory of Ana lingered.

Looking back, I realize that this brief relationship taught me a lot about myself. It taught me that love doesn't always follow the script we expect, and that sometimes, people come into our lives for a brief moment to teach us something important. Even though the relationship was short-lived, it was meaningful, and it left an imprint on my heart.

But like everything else in life, time moved on. And eventually, so did I.

As the days passed after my breakup with Ana, I found myself reflecting on everything we had shared during those few short weeks. It was a bittersweet feeling because while it was over, I couldn't shake the thought of her from my mind. I kept replaying our conversations, our laughter, the way she looked at me, the way we connected. It was everything I had wanted in a relationship, yet somehow, it was fleeting. I had learned that love is not always meant to be forever, and sometimes, it's not even about the end, but the journey.

Back in Sierra Bullones, I tried to focus on my schoolwork, though my thoughts were often elsewhere. I would catch myself daydreaming about her, about how she had made me feel special, about how we had talked about everything under the sun. But there was nothing I could do about it now. What mattered was moving forward.

Despite the deep ache that lingered, I kept my daily routine going. I hung out with my friends, attended school, and focused on what was ahead of me. But deep down, there was still a piece of me that missed Ana. I couldn't forget her, but I knew I had to keep going. I couldn’t let this one heartbreak define me.

The days turned into weeks, and I began to adjust. I had accepted the reality of the situation and was learning how to handle the aftermath of a relationship that ended too soon. I also learned a valuable lesson: sometimes, things don't work out, and it's okay. It's part of life. You can't force something to happen just because you want it badly enough.

However, life had a funny way of surprising me.

It was a few months later when I met someone new, someone completely unexpected. This time, I was a little more cautious, not wanting to rush into anything too soon. I had learned from my past experiences and understood that taking things slow was sometimes the best approach.

Her name was Liza, and she was a year older than me. She had a different energy than Ana more mature and reserved. We met at a local café when I was hanging out with my friends one afternoon. She was sitting at a table alone, reading a book. Something about her caught my attention, and without thinking, I walked over to her.

"Hi," I said, a bit nervous.

She looked up from her book and smiled. "Hey," she replied, her voice soft yet confident. "Can I help you with something?"

I hesitated for a moment, unsure of what to say. I didn't want to come off too forward, but at the same time, I couldn't help myself.

"I was just wondering if you wanted to join us. We're having a coffee break," I said, motioning to my friends.

She raised an eyebrow, clearly surprised by my boldness. But after a beat, she smiled again. "Sure, why not?" she said, closing her book and standing up.

I introduced her to my friends, and the conversation flowed easily. She fit right in with our group, and before I knew it, we were all talking and laughing, as if we had known each other for years. Liza had this effortless charm about her, and I found myself drawn to her. We talked about school, our favorite hobbies, and, of course, books she was an avid reader, which I found fascinating.

After that afternoon, we started to meet more often. We exchanged numbers, texted each other about random things, and began to hang out whenever we could. I couldn't believe how quickly our friendship turned into something more. We would go to the movies, have coffee dates, and even visit local spots around the area. It felt so different from my past relationships, and I appreciated that. It felt natural, with no pressure or expectations.

As we spent more time together, I began to realize something important: I had learned to love again, but this time, I wasn't rushing into anything. It was like a slow burn, a connection that grew stronger with time, and it felt right. The difference with Liza was that I didn't feel the need to rush or put labels on everything. We were both happy with how things were going, and that was all that mattered.

However, there was a part of me that still carried the scars from my previous heartbreak. Every time I felt myself getting closer to Liza, I hesitated. I didn't want to go through another painful breakup. I was scared, unsure of how things would turn out. But Liza was patient with me. She never pushed me, never made me feel pressured. She respected my boundaries and gave me the space I needed.

One afternoon, as we were sitting by the river in Sierra Bullones, watching the sunset, Liza turned to me with a soft smile.

"Ivan, I know we've been spending a lot of time together, and I just wanted to ask you something," she said, her voice gentle.

I looked at her, unsure of what she was about to say. "What is it?"

"Do you think... Do you think there's a possibility for us?" she asked, her eyes searching mine for an answer.

For a moment, I was quiet, my heart pounding in my chest. I had been waiting for this question, but I wasn't sure how to respond. I didn't want to jump into something too quickly, but at the same time, I didn't want to let this moment slip away.

"I think..." I began, taking a deep breath. "I think there's a possibility. But I need to take it slow. I don't want to rush things, not after everything that's happened before."

Liza smiled, her eyes warm and understanding. "I get it. And I'm willing to take it slow too. We don't have to have everything figured out right away."

In that moment, I knew I had made the right decision. Liza and I didn't have to force anything. We could let things unfold at their own pace, and that was more than enough for me.

As we walked back to her house that evening, hand in hand, I couldn't help but feel a sense of peace. For the first time in a long time, I felt like I was exactly where I was supposed to be. Life had a way of testing us, of challenging us with heartbreak and difficult moments, but it also had a way of rewarding us with new beginnings, new connections, and the possibility of love.

And as I looked at Liza, I knew that this was just the beginning of something special. Something that had the potential to last, if we let it.

Chapter 4: The Girl From Rizal

It was during my sophomore year, Grade 9, when I met her. Her name was Mia, and she was from Rizal, Pilar. I remember how it all started, just like any other random Facebook conversation, something that seemed like nothing but turned into something more significant. We were both interested in similar things, and over time, we found ourselves talking more frequently. After a few weeks of chatting, I realized that I was beginning to like her more than just a friend. Her smile, her wit, and her way of making even the most mundane topics seem exciting made me feel something I hadn't felt in a while.

One evening, I gathered the courage to ask her if she would like to be more than just friends. It was a simple question, but my heart raced as I typed it. Her reply came quickly she said yes. I was ecstatic, and it felt like everything was finally falling into place. Mia became my girlfriend, and for a while, everything seemed perfect.

But as with most relationships, there was an underlying tension. I had become possessive, jealous even. There was something about her ex that bothered me. I didn't know why, but the thought of him still being in her life still being part of her past triggered an insecurity in me. I knew I had no reason to feel that way, but I couldn't help myself. Every time she mentioned him, or if I saw anything related to him on her social media, I felt this irrational jealousy rise within me.

One weekend, I decided to visit Mia in Rizal, Pilar. I took three of my close friends along for the trip, and together, we made our way to her house. I remember feeling nervous and excited all at once. Her house wasn't far, and the journey felt longer than it really was because of the anticipation building inside me. When we arrived, Mia was waiting outside, a smile spreading across her face when she saw me. We said our hellos, and soon we were all hanging out, laughing and talking like old friends. But as the day wore on, I noticed something that only heightened my jealousy the way one of my friends kept talking to her, the way they laughed together. My mind was racing, and I didn't like it. I started to feel uncomfortable, uneasy with the situation. It wasn't like I didn't trust her, but something about the way my friend and Mia interacted just didn't sit right with me.

Later that evening, Mia and I went for a walk, holding hands as we made our way down the road. Everything felt a bit surreal, like the world was in perfect sync. But despite the calm, my thoughts were clouded. I couldn't shake the feeling that my friend was spending too much time with her. As we walked back to her house, I realized I had been too quiet, too withdrawn. I didn't want to act possessive, but I couldn't help it. As we sat on the porch, I caught myself staring at my friend for a second too long, wondering if he had been too close to her.

By the end of the night, Mia noticed the change in my demeanor. We said our goodbyes, and I felt a mixture of emotions guilt, confusion, and a lingering sense of jealousy that I couldn't explain. I didn't know why I was acting this way, but it felt like something was slipping away from me. That night, Mia made a decision. She blocked my friend from her social media accounts. I wasn't sure what to think, but I couldn't help but feel a sense of relief. At least I didn't have to worry about him anymore.

Days passed, and we went back to our regular routine texting, chatting, and sharing our day-to-day lives. But as time went on, things began to feel strained. The jealousy that had built up inside me didn't fade; if anything, it grew. Mia's ex was still a presence in my mind, and no matter how much she reassured me, I couldn't shake the thought that I wasn't good enough. That feeling of insecurity gnawed at me more than I was willing to admit.

Then, one day, everything changed.

Her mom found out about us.

I had always known that Mia's relationship with her family was a little complicated, but I never expected it to turn out this way. Her mom, who was very protective of her, had somehow discovered that we were still together despite everything. I never expected her to find out so soon, and when she did, she wasn't pleased.

Mia's mom sent me a message one that I'll never forget. In her message, she told me that she wanted me to break up with her daughter. At first, I thought it was a joke. Maybe she was just being a strict parent. But no, it was very real, and it hit me like a ton of bricks. I was hurt, confused, and angry. Why was she telling me to break up with Mia? We had only been together for a couple of months. I thought we were doing fine, but apparently, her mom didn't see it that way.

I could feel the pressure mounting. I knew that Mia's mom didn't approve of me, and I knew that if I gave in to her request, I might lose her for good. But I wasn't ready to let go. I refused to break up with her, not without a fight. I believed that Mia and I were meant to be together, and I didn't care what her mom thought. I was going to find a way for us to stay connected, to keep the relationship alive.

We started talking in secret, using WhatsApp as our main way of communicating. It was easier that way. Mia's mom couldn't check her messages as easily, and it gave us the privacy we needed to continue our relationship without anyone else interfering. The secrecy, though, came with its own set of challenges. Every conversation felt like a risk, and every message was a reminder that we were doing something wrong. But despite the danger, we couldn't help ourselves.

As time went on, I began to feel the weight of the situation. The secrecy, the constant fear of getting caught it all started to wear me down. And then something unexpected happened.

I lost interest.

It wasn't sudden, but over time, the spark that had once been there began to fade. I don't know if it was the constant pressure from her mom, the jealousy that had taken over, or the fact that I had never fully processed my previous relationship. But I realized that I wasn't feeling the same way about Mia anymore. The connection that once felt so strong was slipping through my fingers, and I couldn't hold on to it anymore.

Eventually, I made the decision. I couldn't keep going like this, not with everything that had happened. I broke up with Mia, though it wasn't easy. I didn't want to hurt her, but I knew it was the right thing to do. I had lost the interest, the drive to make the relationship work. I was no longer the person I had been when I first courted her, and I couldn't pretend anymore.

It was a difficult decision, one that left me with mixed emotions. I felt guilty, sad, and confused. But as time passed, I realized that sometimes, even the best of intentions don't lead to lasting relationships. Not every love story is meant to have a happy ending, and not every relationship survives the challenges it faces. But those experiences shape us, and they help us grow.

After breaking up with Mia, I felt a strange emptiness. There was no more secret texting, no more late-night conversations where we'd talk about everything and nothing at the same time. At first, I thought I'd feel relief. After all, the pressure from her mom and my constant jealousy had made the relationship feel like a battle rather than something enjoyable. But the moment we went our separate ways, I realized how much of an emotional toll it had taken on me. I wasn't entirely sure what had gone wrong, but I knew it wasn't something that could easily be fixed.

In the days following the breakup, I found myself going over everything in my mind, trying to pinpoint the exact moment things had started to unravel. Was it when I became possessive and jealous? Was it when her mom stepped in, demanding we end it? Or was it when I started to lose interest and no longer felt the same spark I had once felt? I couldn't answer these questions with certainty, but the fact remained: the relationship had ended, and I needed to move on.

It wasn't easy. The feeling of guilt kept me awake at night. I kept wondering if I had made the right choice or if I was just running away from something that could have been worked through. I wondered if Mia was feeling the same way or if she had already moved on. In the midst of all this uncertainty, I tried to keep myself busy with school, friends, and the things I enjoyed, but there was always that lingering feeling of doubt.

One day, Mia reached out to me. I was surprised to see her message pop up on my phone, especially after everything that had happened. It was short and simple: "Hey, can we talk?" I hesitated for a moment before I replied. What would she say? Would she ask me why I broke up with her? Would she blame me? I wasn't sure I was ready for that conversation, but I knew I couldn't ignore it. So, I agreed to talk.

We met at a quiet café in the town center a few days later. I was nervous, unsure of what to expect. When she walked in, her expression was calm but distant. She didn't look angry, but there was a sadness in her eyes. I could tell she had been affected by the breakup, just as much as I had. We sat down, and there was an awkward silence between us. Neither of us knew where to start, so I decided to speak first.

"I'm sorry," I said, my voice sincere. "I don't want you to think it was something you did. It's just... I don't know, I wasn't myself toward the end, and I felt like I was losing something. I couldn't handle the pressure anymore."

She nodded, her gaze dropping to the table. "I get it," she said quietly. "It wasn't just you. I think we both started to change, and not for the better. I didn't like how we were with each other near the end, always sneaking around, feeling like we had to hide everything. I just wanted us to be happy, but I don't think that was happening."

I could see the pain in her face, and it hit me harder than I expected. I had never really considered how much the secrecy and the pressure from her mom had affected her. In my mind, I had been so focused on my own feelings, my jealousy, and my insecurity that I hadn't stopped to think about how Mia was dealing with it all. Her mom's disapproval had been a huge burden on her, and she had tried to navigate that while also keeping our relationship intact. In hindsight, I realized just how unfair I had been to her. I had allowed my insecurities to dictate my actions, and I had failed to truly understand her perspective.

We sat there in silence for a few moments, reflecting on what we had said. The conversation wasn't as dramatic as I had feared, but it was emotional. We both acknowledged the mistakes we had made and the things we should have done differently. The tension between us began to dissipate, replaced by a mutual understanding of where things had gone wrong. Neither of us blamed the other, but we both knew that sometimes, relationships just don't work out, no matter how much we want them to.

When we finished our conversation, Mia stood up and gave me a small, bittersweet smile. "I'm glad we talked," she said. "I think we both needed that."

I nodded, feeling a sense of closure that I hadn't realized I needed. The breakup had been painful, but this conversation helped me understand why it had happened. It wasn't anyone's fault; it was simply the result of two people trying to make something work despite the obstacles that life had thrown their way.

After Mia left, I sat there for a while, reflecting on everything we had talked about. I realized that I had learned a valuable lesson from this relationship. I had learned that jealousy and insecurity can ruin something good if you let them take control. I had learned that relationships require trust, understanding, and communication. And most importantly, I had learned that sometimes, it's okay to let go when things aren't working, even if it's hard.

In the weeks that followed, I focused on myself. I didn't rush into another relationship, but I took time to reflect on my own personal growth. I worked on overcoming my insecurities, building my confidence, and learning to trust others again. I also focused on my studies, my friends, and the things that made me happy. I realized that I didn't need to be in a relationship to feel complete, and that the best way to move forward was to take care of myself first.

Mia and I eventually stopped talking. Our paths had diverged, and it seemed like the right time for both of us to move on. I wished her the best, and I hoped that she found someone who could give her the happiness she deserved. I never forgot the lessons I had learned from her, and I carried those lessons with me as I continued on my journey.

As time went on, I became more confident in myself and in my ability to handle whatever life threw my way. Relationships would come and go, but I knew that I was capable of moving forward, no matter how hard it might be. And when the time was right, I would find someone who truly understood me someone who didn't need to be hidden or kept in the shadows. Until then, I would continue to focus on becoming the best version of myself.

Chapter 5: Strains of Love and Unseen Battles

Grade 10 was a year full of mixed emotions, confusing choices, and a lot of self-reflection. When I met her, it was through Facebook. She was from San Jose, Sierra Bullones, but had moved to Laguna. It all started when I noticed her stories on my feed. There was something about the way she captured moments, the way she smiled in the pictures, that made me pause. It wasn't like the usual online interactions I had this was different. She felt real to me, in a way I couldn't explain.

At first, our conversations were light and casual. I'd ask about her day, about the places she loved in Laguna, about her life in general. But as days went by, I couldn't shake the feeling that I wanted to get to know her on a deeper level. She had this kindness about her, a warmth in her messages that made me feel comfortable. We started chatting more regularly, and I found myself waiting for her replies, excited for the next conversation.

Five days passed before I decided to take the plunge. It was something I'd never done before, something that felt so foreign to me but in that moment, I was convinced that I had to act. I wanted to know if there was something between us, if she felt the same way I did. I courted her, asking if she'd give me the chance to know her better.

Her response was hesitant. She didn't immediately say yes, and there was a part of me that felt like I'd just messed up everything. I wasn't sure if I was rushing into things, but the more I thought about her, the more I realized that I wanted to try. She was special, and I couldn't let the opportunity slip away without giving it my best shot.

The next day, to my relief, she said yes. I didn't know what to feel at first was I happy? Nervous? A little bit of both. It wasn't that I didn't want this, but deep down, I was questioning if I had done the right thing. We began messaging nonstop, sharing stories from our past, joking, laughing, and discussing everything from our favorite foods to our most embarrassing moments. I felt like I was finally connecting with someone who understood me, someone I could be myself with.

But there was an undercurrent to our relationship that I couldn't ignore. Something I had never faced before jealousy.

It started small, barely noticeable. A comment from one of her friends here, a shared post there. But it didn't take long for my mind to spiral. Every time someone left a message on her feed or interacted with her in some way, I felt a tightness in my chest, an overwhelming sense of insecurity that I couldn't shake. The thought of anyone else getting too close to her bothered me more than it should have. I tried to brush it off, telling myself it was all in my head, but the jealousy kept growing. It began to consume me, making me doubt everything her intentions, my place in her life, and the future we were building together.

I knew I had to talk to her about it, but I couldn't bring myself to. I didn't want to come off as insecure or possessive, so I kept my feelings to myself. I tried to suppress the jealousy, but it was hard. It was as though it was eating away at me, poisoning the thoughts I had about her and the relationship.

This was the first time I had truly felt the sting of insecurity in a relationship, and I wasn't sure how to handle it. I didn't know what to do with the feelings, and I didn't know how to make them go away. My thoughts became a constant battle, unsure of where the relationship was headed and if I could truly trust the bond we were starting to build.

After everything moved so quickly, and I finally had her in my life, I was filled with a mixture of joy and unease. There was this undeniable connection between us, something that made every conversation feel meaningful, but my insecurities continued to hold me captive. Despite all the sweetness we shared, the constant battle with my own jealousy had started to take a toll.

As I settled into my work in Cebu, I could feel the distance between us. Not just in terms of physical space, but emotionally as well. My thoughts started to get tangled in a web of doubt. Being in a new place, away from the comfort of her presence, gave me too much time to overthink. It didn't help that she was constantly interacting with people especially her friends. One particular friend had caught my eye in a way that I couldn't ignore, and that friend's presence on her Facebook, his comments, and the way they seemed to share a bond made my heart race with envy.

I started reading between the lines of every post, every comment, trying to decipher hidden meanings that weren't even there. The jealousy was irrational, but I couldn't stop it. Every time I saw her talking to him or any of her other friends, the dark cloud of insecurity would swirl in my mind, and it made me lash out.

One night, after a particularly long fight, I found myself standing in front of my phone, staring at the screen, waiting for her to reply. I was hurt by something she had said in passing something about her friend and I couldn't let it go. The floodgates of frustration opened, and before I knew it, the words I sent her were filled with anger and accusations.

I could feel the tension on the other end of the conversation. She didn't respond right away, and I knew I had pushed her too far. The silence that followed felt deafening, and I regretted everything. But it was too late. The damage had already been done.

The next day, we tried to talk, but the conversation felt different. Every word seemed to carry the weight of unresolved issues. There were too many unsaid things between us, too much bitterness that I couldn't wash away. The foundation of our relationship was starting to crack, and I could feel it slipping through my fingers.

This went on for weeks. We'd have our good days, but they felt overshadowed by the constant arguments. We were growing apart, but I couldn't let go. I wanted to fix things, but every attempt felt like we were just circling the same toxic patterns over and over again.

Then, it all came crashing down. We had another fight, one that was far more intense than anything we'd experienced before. I was consumed by my jealousy, my insecurity, and my fears of losing her to someone else. It all erupted during a conversation, and this time, it was too much. She broke down, and I could hear the sadness in her voice.

"I don't know what to do anymore," she said. "I feel like I'm walking on eggshells, and I can't keep doing this."

Her words hit me harder than anything. It was the first time she had truly expressed how much my actions were affecting her. She didn't want to be with someone who was constantly questioning her loyalty or love.

It was in that moment that I realized how badly I had messed up. The jealousy that had consumed me, the fear of losing her, had pushed her away. The promises I had made to her and her family about not hurting her had fallen apart. I had become someone I didn't want to be, someone she couldn't trust.

After that, we both knew that something had to change, but it was too late. The damage was irreversible. I tried to hold on, but she knew it was time for us to end things.

The day we broke up, it felt like the ground beneath me had shifted, and I was left standing in an unfamiliar place. I had spent so much time trying to control everything, trying to hold on to something that I feared slipping away, that I never stopped to consider what she needed from me. Her sadness lingered in my mind long after the conversation ended, and I could feel the weight of my mistakes pressing against my chest.

After the breakup, I found myself lost in a sea of guilt and regret. I had hurt her. Worse, I had hurt myself. I had been so consumed by my own insecurities that I had overlooked the most important thing trust. Trust was the foundation of any relationship, and I had let my jealousy tear it down.

There were days when I couldn't focus on anything. My work in Cebu, which had once given me purpose, felt hollow. I couldn't shake the image of her face when she cried, when I had said things I didn't mean. The moments we had shared together, the sweet messages, the laughter, and the late-night conversations all of it seemed to fade into the background. I had destroyed something beautiful, and there was no going back.

I tried to reach out to her again, but it was clear that she had moved on. Her responses were polite but distant. The warmth that had once been there between us had evaporated. It was like talking to a stranger who was once someone I knew so intimately.

One night, after days of constant overthinking, I decided to call her. The phone rang for what felt like an eternity, and when she finally answered, her voice was calm. Too calm.

"Ivan, what is it?" she asked, a hint of exhaustion in her tone.

I could feel my heart pounding as I struggled to find the right words. "I just wanted to say... I'm sorry. For everything. I messed up, and I know it. I know I hurt you."

There was a long pause, and I could hear her breathing softly on the other end. "I know you're sorry," she replied. "But sometimes, sorry doesn't fix things. It's too late for that."

Those words hit me like a cold wave, and I felt a lump form in my throat. "I don't know what to do without you," I admitted, my voice cracking. "I can't change the past, but I'll always regret how things ended."

"I know," she said, her voice softer now. "But I have to let go. You have to let go too."

I knew she was right. We both needed to move on. But it didn't make it any easier. There was a part of me that still clung to the hope that we could fix things, that we could somehow turn back time and undo the damage. But in reality, that wasn't possible. The things I had done, the choices I had made, had set us on a path that could no longer be changed.

After the call, I felt numb. There was no immediate relief, no sense of closure. It felt like the end of something that had once been so important, and I was left to pick up the pieces of my heart, which felt shattered beyond repair.

The days that followed were some of the hardest I had ever faced. I spent long hours reflecting on the relationship and my mistakes. I wondered if I could ever find someone else who would love me the way she had, and I realized that I had taken her love for granted. It was a painful realization, one that left me questioning myself and the person I had become.

But in the silence that followed, I also learned something valuable. It took me a long time to come to terms with it, but I finally realized that love isn't just about holding on to someone it's about giving them the space to grow, to be themselves, and to trust them. I had tried to hold on too tight, and in doing so, I had smothered the very thing I had wanted to protect.

I took time for myself after the breakup, focusing on my personal growth and reflection. I worked on healing, learning to control my jealousy, and coming to terms with the fact that I couldn't change the past. I also realized that relationships, like anything in life, require balance. Trust, understanding, and space are just as important as affection and shared moments. I didn't have all the answers, but I was determined to learn from this experience.

The pain of the breakup never fully disappeared. There were still moments when I would think about her, about the way we were, and it would hurt all over again. But with time, the wound began to heal. Slowly, I began to understand that it wasn't the end of my story. It was just another chapter, one that had taught me valuable lessons.

Life after heartbreak feels like walking through a foggy landscape each step uncertain, the path ahead unclear. I had to find a way to move forward, even when it felt like I was leaving a part of myself behind. The weight of the breakup lingered, but I refused to let it define me.

In the weeks that followed, I immersed myself in work and personal growth. I needed something to fill the void, to keep my mind occupied. The routine became my solace: waking up early, setting small goals for the day, and pushing through each hour with purpose. Slowly, the fog began to lift, and I found a semblance of clarity.

One of the hardest parts of moving forward was breaking the cycle of overthinking. Late at night, when everything was quiet, my mind would replay moments from the relationship like an endless reel. I remembered the good times, the laughter, and the shared dreams. But I also remembered the arguments, the misunderstandings, and the way it all fell apart.

To break free from these thoughts, I started journaling. Writing became an outlet for my emotions, a way to process the pain and confusion that lingered. I wrote letters I'd never send, conversations I wished we'd had, and reflections on the person I wanted to become.

As the days turned into weeks and the weeks into months, I began to focus on rebuilding myself. I enrolled in a few online courses, hoping to learn new skills that would not only improve my career but also give me a sense of accomplishment. Each small victory, whether it was mastering a concept or completing an assignment, gave me the confidence I had lost.

I also reconnected with old friends. For so long, I had been so consumed by my relationship that I had distanced myself from the people who cared about me. Rebuilding those connections reminded me that I wasn't alone, that there were people who still valued me despite my flaws.

Fitness became another important part of my journey. It wasn't just about improving my physical health, it was about discipline and self-respect. Every run, every workout session, felt like a small step toward reclaiming control over my life. The sweat and exhaustion were cathartic, a way to release the pent-up frustration and sadness that I had carried for so long.

It's funny how life has a way of surprising us when we least expect it. One afternoon, while I was running errands in town, I spotted her. She was walking with a friend, her laughter carried by the wind. For a moment, I froze. My heart raced, and a flood of emotions washed over me, nostalgia, longing, and a pang of sadness.

But this time, I didn't feel the urge to approach her or say anything. Instead, I stood there, quietly observing her from a distance. She seemed happy, and that brought me a strange sense of comfort. Seeing her like that made me realize that she had moved on, and I could, too.

Letting go isn't a single act; it's a process, one that requires patience and resilience. I learned to accept that some people come into our lives to teach us lessons, to shape us into better versions of ourselves, even if they aren't meant to stay.

I forgave myself for my mistakes and forgave her for the pain we both endured. It wasn't easy, but it was necessary. Holding onto resentment would only keep me chained to the past, and I didn't want to live like that anymore.

As time passed, the pain of the breakup dulled, replaced by a quiet strength. I was no longer the person I had been when we were together. I had grown, learned, and healed in ways I never thought possible.

Looking back, I realized that our relationship, though flawed, had been a crucial part of my journey. It taught me about love, vulnerability, and the importance of trust. It also taught me that sometimes, the most profound growth comes from the most painful experiences.

Now, as I stand on the threshold of a new chapter, I carry those lessons with me. The scars remain, but they no longer define me. They are reminders of where I've been and how far I've come.

IN THE MONTHS THAT followed, healing felt like a distant dream. I started to accept that there wouldn't be an "aha" moment when everything magically felt better. Healing wasn't a straight road; it was a winding path filled with setbacks and breakthroughs.

I spent a lot of time rediscovering who I was outside the relationship. For so long, my identity had been intertwined with "us." I was no longer just Ivan, I had been someone's boyfriend, someone's confidant, someone's partner in everything. Now, I had to figure out what it meant to be just me again.

I found solace in the little things: the routine of my daily runs, the books I had been meaning to read, and even the quiet mornings spent sipping coffee while the world outside came alive. It was in these small, quiet moments that I started to feel like myself again.

One of the unexpected blessings of this period was the revival of old friendships. People I hadn't spoken to in years suddenly reached out, either because they had heard about the breakup or simply because they missed me.

There was Mark, a childhood friend who now lived in Cebu. He invited me to join his hiking group. At first, I hesitated. The idea of being around people felt overwhelming, but something inside me urged me to say yes.

The first hike was a revelation. As we climbed higher and higher, the city faded away, replaced by the serene beauty of the mountains. The fresh air, the sound of birds, and the laughter of my fellow hikers felt like a balm for my soul. For the first time in months, I felt alive.

Through these hikes, I realized that healing didn't have to be a solitary journey. Sometimes, the people around us their kindness, their stories, their laughter can help us find pieces of ourselves that we thought were lost.

Another crucial part of my healing journey was confronting the insecurities that had plagued me throughout the relationship. I started therapy, something I had always been hesitant about. The first few sessions were uncomfortable opening up to a stranger about my deepest fears and regrets wasn't easy.

But slowly, I began to see the patterns in my behavior. My jealousy and need for control weren't about her they were about me. They stemmed from my fear of abandonment, from the wounds of my past that I had never properly addressed.

My therapist helped me see that it was okay to be vulnerable, that trust wasn't about guaranteeing someone would never leave it was about having faith in the connection and accepting that nothing in life is certain.

One evening, as I was sorting through old photos, I came across a picture of us. We were sitting by the beach, the sun setting behind us, and our smiles were wide and genuine. For a moment, I felt a pang of sadness.

But then, something shifted. Instead of longing for what was, I felt gratitude. That relationship, as painful as it had been, had given me so much joy, growth, and lessons I would carry with me for the rest of my life.

That night, I wrote in my journal: "Letting go isn't about forgetting; it's about honoring what was and making space for what could be."

About a year after the breakup, I met someone new. Her name was Mia, and she was everything I wasn't calm, patient, and unshaken by life's ups and downs. We met at a seminar about entrepreneurship, a topic I had thrown myself into as part of my self-improvement journey.

Mia wasn't just kind; she was understanding. From the beginning, I was honest about my past and the mistakes I had made. Instead of judging me, she listened. She taught me that love didn't have to be complicated or full of drama. It could be steady, supportive, and kind.

Our connection grew slowly, built on a foundation of trust and mutual respect. She helped me see that I was capable of being a better partner not perfect, but better.

As Mia and I grew closer, I found myself reflecting on the contrast between this relationship and the one I had lost. It wasn't that one was better than the other, they were simply different. With Mia, I didn't feel the need to control or overthink. Instead, I felt a quiet sense of security that I hadn't known before.

But it wasn't all smooth sailing. I had to confront the ghosts of my past constantly. Every now and then, I would catch myself doubting Mia's intentions, wondering if I was enough for her, or fearing that I might repeat my mistakes.

One evening, as we sat in a cozy café overlooking Cebu's bustling streets, I decided to open up to her about these fears.

"Mia," I began hesitantly, stirring the remnants of my coffee, "there's something I need to tell you. Sometimes, I feel... scared. Not of you, but of myself. I don't want to hurt you the way I've hurt someone before."

She reached across the table and placed her hand over mine. "Ivan, the fact that you're aware of your past mistakes and willing to talk about them says a lot about who you are now. You've grown, and I see that. But you don't have to be perfect. You just have to be honest."

Her words hit me like a gentle wave, washing away the lingering doubts. She was right. I didn't need to be perfect, I just needed to keep learning, keep trying, and keep being honest with myself and the people around me.

Over time, I started to rebuild my life piece by piece. My work in Cebu became more than just a way to pass the time, it became a passion. I threw myself into new projects, finding satisfaction in creating something meaningful.

I also rekindled my love for writing, something I had set aside during the turbulence of my previous relationship. I started journaling again, capturing not just my thoughts but also the lessons I had learned along the way.

Mia encouraged me to share my writings with others, and before long, I found myself posting short reflections on social media. To my surprise, they resonated with people. Messages poured in from strangers who had gone through similar experiences, thanking me for putting into words the feelings they couldn't express.

One message, in particular, stood out. It was from a young man in Manila who had just gone through a breakup. He wrote:

"Your posts helped me realize that I'm not alone in feeling this way. Thank you for sharing your story, it's given me hope."

For the first time in a long time, I felt like my pain had a purpose.

About two years after the breakup, I received a message from her, the girl from Rizal. It was short and to the point:

"I hope you're doing well. I wanted to let you know that I've forgiven you. I hope you've found peace."

Reading those words felt like a weight had been lifted off my chest. I realized that I had been holding onto guilt, even after all the progress I had made. Her forgiveness wasn't something I had expected, but it was a gift I would always cherish.

I replied, thanking her and wishing her happiness. It wasn't a conversation meant to rekindle anything, it was simply two people acknowledging their shared history and moving forward.

As I sat on the balcony of my apartment that evening, watching the city lights flicker in the distance, I felt a sense of closure I hadn't known I needed.

Life had a way of teaching us the lessons we needed to learn, even if it took heartbreak and struggle to get there. I had learned to love again not just someone else, but also myself.

With Mia by my side, a renewed sense of purpose in my work, and a deeper understanding of what it meant to truly connect with someone, I was ready to face whatever came next.

Because love, I realized, wasn't just about finding the right person. It was about becoming the right person for yourself and others. And in that journey, I had discovered a strength I never knew I had.

Chapter 6: Unspoken Words and Lost Chances

It was a quiet afternoon when I first saw her. My brother had mentioned her once or twice before, but it wasn't until that moment that I realized how much I had admired her from a distance. She was the girl I had silently crushed on since I was in seventh grade, and now, after everything had changed with my previous relationships, the feeling resurfaced with intensity. I had never had the courage to talk to her before, but this time, things were different.

After my first breakup, I found myself thinking about her more often. She was in my brother's class, and every time I saw her, I couldn't help but feel a flutter in my chest. Her smile, her laugh, the way she carried herself they were all etched in my mind. So, after some time of hesitation, I decided to take the leap. I added her on Facebook, and to my surprise, she accepted.

It felt like a small victory, even if it was just the beginning. I texted her first, nervously, unsure of what would happen. But she replied, and the conversation began. We talked about everything and nothing, and with every text, it felt like we were slowly getting to know each other. I didn't expect much, but there was a spark, a connection that I couldn't ignore. I started going to her classroom more often, pretending it was a coincidence, but deep down, I knew it was more than that. Every moment spent with her felt significant, like a step closer to something I had always wanted.

Weeks passed, and I gathered the courage to confess. I wasn't expecting much just wanted to be honest with her. To my surprise, she told me that she liked me too. My heart skipped a beat. I had been holding onto this crush for so long, and now, in this moment, I realized that maybe it wasn't just a dream.

But then, reality set in. She told me that she wasn't ready for a relationship. It was crushing, but I understood. I respected her decision, and instead of pushing her, I waited. She allowed me to wait for her, and I was willing to do it. Every time we talked, I cherished those moments, hoping that one day, she would be ready.

One of the happiest moments of my life happened during a high school game at school. I went to watch her and her friends play, and amidst the chaos of the game, something beautiful happened. We ended up holding hands, and though it was part of the game, it felt like so much more. My heart raced, and I couldn't help but smile, knowing that maybe just maybe this could turn into something real.

But then came the late-night message that would change everything.

It was 1 a.m. when she texted me out of nowhere: "Hallo, am scared hahaha, yatia nakamata ko nya Di naku katug balik ani huhu 😭 cute lagi ni, samoka mani, feel naku gadamgo ko haha, laina akong damgo oy waman ko kaila adto nila, sige bye." At first, I didn't know what to make of it. Was she just being playful, or was there something deeper she was trying to say? I didn't know, but the uncertainty lingered.

We had a conversation that night, joking about crushes, laughing about the idea of secrets, and sharing little moments that made everything feel like a game. But there was something in her responses that hinted at hesitation. When I asked her if she had a crush on me, she danced around the question, laughing it off, saying it was a secret. I wanted her to be honest, to tell me how she really felt, but the moment slipped away with a joke. I let it go, but a part of me couldn't help but wonder.

As the days passed, things began to change. We walked together after school, sometimes hand in hand, and I thought maybe we were getting closer. But then, one day, I couldn't hold it in anymore. I told her I loved her. It felt right in that moment, but the reaction was not what I expected. She seemed uncomfortable. The words that followed felt heavy in the air between us, and I knew something had shifted. Our misunderstanding started to grow from that moment on.

Soon, we stopped talking, and it didn't take long for her to block me. The weight of everything crashed down on me. I didn't know what went wrong. I was lost. I even considered transferring to another school, but in the end, I chose to go to Cebu instead, hoping it would help me forget and move on.

I thought I was ready to let go, but the feeling didn't fade. No matter how far I went, how much I tried to move on, she stayed with me. I couldn't get her out of my mind. I realized that I wasn't just waiting for her, I was holding onto something that wasn't mine to hold onto anymore. The reality of it all hit me hard. She had blocked me, and we were no longer in contact, but my heart still yearned for something that had never fully been given a chance to bloom.

In Cebu, I threw myself into work, trying to bury my feelings in busy routines. But even in the busyness, her memory lingered like an unfinished song. I kept thinking about her late-night message, the way she joked, the way she hesitated when we talked about our feelings. I couldn't understand why things ended the way they did, but I knew I had made my mistakes. I had pushed her when she wasn't ready, and in doing so, I had hurt both of us. I had to accept that.

The hardest part was admitting to myself that I was still waiting for her, even though I knew deep down that she had moved on. But I couldn't help it. I still held onto the hope that one day, we might cross paths again, that maybe this time, things would work out. But as time passed, I knew that I had to stop waiting and start living.

I tried to convince myself that I needed to let go, but it wasn't easy. The memories of us together, the laughter, the holding hands, the conversations weighed heavily on my heart. I kept wondering what could have been, what we could have built if I had been patient, if I hadn't pushed too hard.

But time has a way of healing wounds, and slowly, I started to move forward. I focused on my own growth, on learning from my mistakes, and on becoming a better version of myself. Maybe, just maybe, one day, I would be able to look back at this chapter of my life with peace, knowing that I had learned what I needed to learn.

But for now, I was still waiting. Still hoping. Still wondering if our paths would cross again.

The years went by, but I never really let go. I continued to hold on to the memories of her, of the girl who had made my heart race and my world feel alive. I don't know if it was love or just the feeling of being deeply connected to someone, but either way, I never truly moved on.

I kept thinking about her, even in the quiet moments. There were times when I wondered if she ever thought about me too, if she remembered those late-night texts, those walks together, those moments that seemed so fleeting but meant so much to me. But I couldn't ask her. I couldn't reach out, because the past had already been written. And no matter how much I wished for a different ending, I knew it wasn't something I could change.

And so, I waited. I waited for the day when I would finally find peace with what had happened, when I could let go of the girl I had loved and the life we never had. It wasn't easy, but it was the only choice I had left.

Chapter 7: The Rollercoaster of a Long-Distance Relationship

It was during my 11th grade when everything changed. I had always been a focused at the gym, balancing gyml and the usual teenage challenges, but then something unexpected happened. I met someone who would alter the course of my life, someone I couldn't ignore.

It wasn't like any of the other crushes I had in the past. This was different. It all began when I got into a relationship with my last girlfriend, the one who left a deep mark on me. We met through Facebook of all places and our connection began when I replied to one of her stories. At first, it was nothing more than a casual comment. But something about that conversation clicked, and we began chatting more regularly.

I had been in relationships before, but this felt different. I had been in love with the idea of being in love, but with her, I felt an emotional pull that I couldn't explain. And as our friendship grew, so did my feelings. After some time, I gathered the courage to confess to her how I felt, and to my surprise, she confessed her feelings back.

But despite the deep connection we had, things weren't easy. We lived in different countries she in Germany, me in the Philippines and the distance between us made our relationship a constant challenge. There were moments of joy, but also many misunderstandings. These small arguments felt like obstacles, but they never deterred us from trying to make things work.

It was one of those mornings where the world seemed to wake up a little differently. My phone lit up with her name, and my curiosity turned into disbelief as I read her message. It wasn't just any message it was the message. The one I'd been hoping for, waiting for, and dreaming of for the past five months.

"Hey van or would I say boo. I may not be a perfect girl ky yk na masuko ko HAHAH, but u still understand me and u can handle my maldita things lol. Pero yk I'm not a maldita girl man jud if mapikon rako maka say ko og words ng di maayo and sorry abt that. Ik that yk na it's hard for me to show my love jud especially na layo. You don't know me sa person jud ky sa person I'm very different.

Idk how to write that much words so ayaw ka surprise HAHA. Btaw mao nani akung iingon, uve been waiting for 5 months now and I really appreciate it boo thank u very much for staying basig it's hard man jud. Ok mao najud ni. I'm accepting u as my bf na like boyfriend aguyy gi kilig ni bah HAHAHA. What would I call u love ning ky cringe nang boo I think HAHAH basta mao nani.

I love you boo or love.

Piro di nako e change ang name nimo ani sa messenger ha cuz I like it ayaw ko pugsa dzungss, ky basig bawion nako akung gipang ingon HAHAH jk.

Basta ayaw kalimti atung monthsary 27 dzungsss ha bantay ka HAHAH."

As I read her message, I was taken aback. I could feel the butterflies in my stomach as her words sunk in. She had accepted me. After months of waiting, of late-night conversations, misunderstandings, and moments of vulnerability, she had finally said yes.

Her words weren't perfect they didn't have to be. That was the beauty of it. She had expressed herself in her own way, with humor, honesty, and a bit of playful teasing. It was quintessentially her.

The past five months hadn't been easy. There were moments when I doubted if this would ever happen, moments when the distance between us felt insurmountable. But I held on because I knew she was worth it.

Her "maldita" ways, as she called them, were never a problem for me. They were just a part of who she was a fiery, passionate person who cared deeply but didn't always know how to show it. I knew that underneath her quick temper was a heart full of love, even if she struggled to express it.

Her message wasn't just an acceptance it was a glimpse into her heart. She acknowledged her flaws, apologized for her outbursts, and admitted that showing love wasn't easy for her. But despite all that, she was willing to take a chance on us.

Her playful tone, her teasing about what to call me, and her insistence on keeping my name unchanged on Messenger made me laugh. It was so her to mix heartfelt emotions with humor.

And then there was the part that made my heart race: "I'm accepting u as my bf na like boyfriend."

The way she phrased it, the excitement in her words it was perfect. I could picture her blushing as she typed it, maybe even giggling to herself.

I knew I had to respond carefully. I didn't want to overwhelm her, but I also wanted her to know how much this meant to me.

"Good morning, love. Or should I still call you boo? HAHA. I honestly didn't expect to wake up to this, but wow, you've just made my day, my week, my entire year.

Thank you for accepting me, for trusting me, and for letting me into your life. I know it hasn't been easy for you, and I appreciate everything you've done to make this work, even when it felt hard.

I don't mind what you call me love, boo, dzungsss anything sounds perfect when it's coming from you. And don't worry, I'll never forget our monthsary on the 27th. Bantay ka if I do HAHA.

I love you too, love. And I'll do everything I can to make you feel that, even from miles away."

Her message marked the beginning of something new. It wasn't just about becoming official it was about moving forward together, despite the distance, despite the challenges.

That day, I felt a renewed sense of purpose. Every sacrifice, every late-night call, every argument, it was all worth it because now, I had her.

I couldn't wait to see where this journey would take us. For now, all I could do was cherish the moment and look forward to the 27th, our first monthsary as a couple.

The first few months were a whirlwind of emotions. There were days when it felt like everything was going perfectly, and then there were times when it seemed like we couldn't stop fighting. I didn't know how to handle the distance, and it led me to make mistakes. I became toxic, driven by insecurities and trust issues that I couldn't shake off. I wasn't proud of the way I acted, but at the time, it felt like I was doing everything I could to hold onto the relationship. Unfortunately, the more I held on, the more it pushed her away.

I didn't know how to control my emotions, and it led to a cycle of misunderstanding and constant tension. She was patient with me at first, but over time, it became too much for her. She decided to break up with me, and I was left heartbroken, devastated.

In the early morning, while I was still half-asleep, my phone buzzed with a message notification. It was from her. My heart raced as I unlocked my phone. The timestamp showed that it was evening in Germany. Her message, long and heartfelt, caught me off guard.

*"Hey, I just wanna say sorry. Sorry if I messed up sometimes and I'm truly sorry. I'm sorry because you have to deal with me. I'm sorry I made you feel that way, like feeling na I didn't give you much assurance. I talk like, as if... idk, I just can't handle it. But you still understand me. We both have mistakes; I know that, samot na misunderstanding, murag hobby na nato na bah HAHAH.

I'm not good at giving words, like yk na I'm not that kind of person. I don't have words of affection as a love language, makita nmn diba HAHAHA. Pero tbh lng, di man ko kanonay maka ingon nimo og mga words na imong ginahan, like sometimes ipa-feel nako nimo na I don't love u or care about u. But yk I do love u and care about u. Sometimes I just need time to think ky I can't, samot na what happened w my dad.

Sometimes I feel guilty. Basta, sorry if I'm like this, like dali masuko or for u na it's maldita. Murag lahi man namo na HAHAH ng maldita bah. Btaw, I'm thankful to have u and that u understand me a lot jud��."*

As I read her message, I couldn't help but smile. It was her, in all her raw and unfiltered honesty. She wasn't someone who expressed her emotions often, but when she did, it came with a sincerity that hit me deeply.

She had always been the type to get easily frustrated when I made mistakes. At times, I felt like I was walking on eggshells, careful not to upset her. But beyond her sharp words and quick temper, there was a sweetness, a love that she couldn't always articulate but was always there.

Her message was a mix of apology and gratitude a rare moment when she let her guard down and allowed me to see the vulnerable side of her. It wasn't easy for her to admit that she struggled, that she felt guilty for how she acted or how she communicated her feelings.

I could feel the weight of her words, especially when she mentioned her dad. She had been through so much, and sometimes her emotions got the better of her. She didn't mean to hurt me; I knew that. It was just her way of coping, her way of handling the rollercoaster of life.

For a long-distance relationship, moments like this were crucial. They reminded me why I was fighting for us despite the miles that separated us. Her words, though imperfect, carried the love and appreciation she had for me.

Her mention of our misunderstandings made me chuckle. It was true arguments had become almost a regular occurrence between us. It wasn't that we didn't love each other; it was just that the distance magnified every small disagreement. Misunderstandings turned into full-blown arguments because we couldn't see each other's expressions or feel the comfort of a hug after a fight.

But this message showed me something important. She wasn't just acknowledging our challenges; she was taking responsibility for her part in them. And in doing so, she was giving me the reassurance I needed that despite our ups and downs, she cared deeply about us.

I took a moment to collect my thoughts before responding. I wanted her to feel the same sincerity she had shown me.

*"Thank you for this, love. Reading your message made me smile. I know you're not the type to say these things often, so it means a lot to me. I understand everything, even the times when you get mad or act maldita. I know it's not easy for you, especially with what's happened.

I want you to know that I see your efforts, and I appreciate them. We've had our fair share of arguments, but I've never doubted your love. You don't always have to say it with words, I can feel it in the little things you do, even from miles away.

I'm thankful for you too, for staying with me despite my own mistakes. We're not perfect, but we're learning together, and that's what matters. I love you."*

In the weeks that followed, I fell into a dark place. I couldn't handle the idea of losing her. My emotions consumed me, and I started to think that the world would be better off without me. There were moments when I thought of ending it all moments when the pain seemed unbearable. But even then, I didn't want to lose her. I wanted to make things right.

Somehow, despite everything, we managed to get back together. I promised her I would change. I swore I would work on myself, fix the issues that I had caused. But it wasn't enough. I couldn't break the cycle.

We broke up and got back together again and again, and every time, I thought it would be the last time. But there we were, trying to salvage something that seemed impossible to fix.

While filled with love and laughter, wasn't without its challenges. I was deeply insecure, and those insecurities often manifested in ways that strained our connection. Long-distance relationships demand trust, and while she was patient and understanding, my paranoia and trust issues created unnecessary tension between us.

I vividly remember one particular incident. She mentioned she was heading out with friends. To most people, this would be harmless, but my mind was a battlefield of overthinking. I asked where she was going and for every little detail about her outing. However, that wasn't enough for me.

Driven by paranoia, I went to Google Maps, piecing together information about the places she had mentioned. I started tracking her movements based on vague clues she had given me. It wasn't hacking, but it was obsessive an invasion of her privacy disguised as "concern." When she returned, I proudly confronted her, telling her exactly which store she had visited.

Her reaction was a mix of disbelief and anger. She was shocked that I had gone to such lengths, and rightfully so. "How could you do that?" she asked, her voice trembling with frustration. "Do you really not trust me at all?"

At that moment, I realized how much I had crossed a line. But instead of apologizing or backing down, my insecurities took over. I argued that I was only trying to protect our relationship, not seeing how my actions were pushing her away.

This wasn't an isolated incident. My constant need for reassurance, combined with my inability to let go of my fears, led to frequent arguments. Every time she went out, I interrogated her. I demanded answers to questions that had no reason to be asked. It was exhausting for both of us.

Our fights escalated to the point where she became increasingly frustrated and distant. She tried to reassure me, but my actions made it clear that her words weren't enough for me. My jealousy and controlling behavior overshadowed the love and effort she put into the relationship.

Finally, after yet another argument sparked by my distrust, she couldn't take it anymore. "I can't do this, Ivan," she said, tears streaming down her face during one of our video calls. "I love you, but this isn't healthy for either of us. I feel like I'm constantly being judged and controlled."

Her words hit me like a ton of bricks. Deep down, I knew she was right. I had let my fears and insecurities poison something beautiful. But instead of taking responsibility, I lashed out in frustration, unable to accept that I was the root cause of our problems.

That fight was the breaking point. We ended the call, and the silence that followed was deafening. For days, I tried to reach out to her, but she was done. She blocked me on social media, cutting off all contact. The relationship that I had fought so hard to keep, the love that I had cherished, was gone because of my inability to trust and my toxic behavior.

In the aftermath, I was consumed by regret. I replayed every argument, every moment I had doubted her, and every time I had let my insecurities control me. The realization of what I had lost was unbearable. She had been patient, understanding, and loving, but I had taken it all for granted.

As painful as it was, this experience became a harsh but necessary lesson for me. Trust is the foundation of any relationship, and without it, love cannot thrive. My mistakes had cost me someone truly special, and I vowed to never let my insecurities ruin something so precious again.

Eventually, the emotional toll became too much for her to bear. She wanted out. I remember that moment like it was yesterday. She told me she couldn't handle it anymore. It was the hardest thing I had ever heard, and the thought of losing her for good was something I couldn't fathom. I tried to change, but I was still battling my own demons. It felt like I was slowly losing myself in this toxic cycle, and it seemed like she was too. That was the moment I reached my lowest point.

The pain from that breakup was so intense that I felt like I was suffocating. I remember crying for hours, unable to stop the tears that seemed to flow endlessly. The anger, the pain, the regret all of it overwhelmed me. And even though I didn't want to admit it, the toxic thoughts crept in again. I didn't know how to live without her.

At my lowest, I became even more desperate. My behavior became erratic. I didn't know how to control the pain that seemed to consume me. I pushed her further away, and eventually, she blocked me. That was it. I was cut off from the one person who had meant everything to me.

I didn't know what to do with myself. Every part of me wanted to reach out, to apologize, to make things right. But I knew that I had already gone too far. I had ruined everything, and now, she was gone.

After our breakup, I found myself unable to let go completely. My heart ached with the weight of what I had lost, and I couldn't stop thinking about her. I knew she had moved on, or at least was trying to, but I couldn't bring myself to accept it.

In those moments of longing, I turned to her best friend. I didn't tell her best friend everything, but I would often ask, "How is she doing?" The answers were always short and neutral, as if to keep from giving me any hope. Still, even hearing about her, no matter how brief, felt like a lifeline.

One day, in a moment of desperation, I recorded a voice message for her best friend to deliver to her. It was in German language I had been learning quietly during our relationship. She had no idea I could speak or understand it, but I had been practicing for months, inspired by her culture and wanting to connect with her on a deeper level.

I hesitated before sending it, unsure if it was the right thing to do. My words, though simple, carried all the emotions I had bottled up since the breakup:

"Ich weiß, dass ich Fehler gemacht habe. Ich habe dich verletzt, und es tut mir leid. Ich vermisse dich, mehr als ich sagen kann. Du warst mein Zuhause, und jetzt fühle ich mich verloren."

Translated, it meant: "I know I made mistakes. I hurt you, and I'm sorry. I miss you, more than I can say. You were my home, and now I feel lost."

I asked her best friend to deliver the message without mentioning it was from me. At first, her best friend hesitated, unsure if it was a good idea. But after some persuasion, she agreed.

Days passed, and I heard nothing. I started to regret sending the message, wondering if it had made things worse. Did she recognize my voice? Did she even care? The silence was unbearable.

Eventually, her best friend told me that she had played the message for her. "She listened," she said. "But she didn't say much after that. She just looked... sad."

Hearing that both comforted and crushed me. On one hand, it meant she still felt something, but on the other, it reminded me that my actions had caused her pain. I wanted so badly to fix things, but I knew deep down that some wounds couldn't be undone with words, no matter how heartfelt.

From then on, I tried to step back. I realized that constantly reaching out, even through indirect means, wasn't fair to her or to me. She deserved to heal and move on, just as I needed to learn to let go.

But even as I tried to focus on my own healing, the memory of her lingered. The message I sent was my last attempt to reach her, my final way of saying what I couldn't during our time together.

It was both a goodbye and a confession a way of acknowledging my mistakes while also expressing the love I still held for her.

But then, something unexpected happened. Four months later, we crossed paths in the most random of places Unitop, in Tagbilaran.

It was the most surreal moment of my life. There we were, standing in the same store, in the same aisle. We locked eyes for a brief moment, and in that instant, time seemed to stop. We were both shocked. I could see it in her eyes she didn't expect to see me there, and neither did I. I didn't know how to react. My heart was racing, and I could feel my palms sweating.

Without thinking, I quickly turned and walked out of the store. I didn't want to face her, not like this not after everything that had happened between us. I went outside and waited, hoping that maybe she would leave without noticing me. But I kept watching her from the window. I knew she was still inside.

I didn't know why I acted the way I did. Maybe I was scared. Maybe I was ashamed. But I didn't want to face her. I was terrified of what she might say, of the disappointment I knew would be in her eyes.

After a few minutes, she left the store with her friends. I was still standing outside, frozen in place, unsure of what to do next. As I watched her walk away, I realized how much I had missed her, how much I still cared about her.

But I didn't have the courage to approach her. Instead, I did something even stranger. Later that day, I went to Alturas with some friends to buy groceries. I thought I had gotten away from her. But fate had other plans.

As I was walking through the store, I saw her again. This time, she was walking with her friends, and I pretended to be asleep. I couldn't face her. I couldn't deal with the emotions that seeing her stirred up inside me. I had no idea what she was thinking, but I couldn't take the chance of talking to her again.

After the encounter at Alturas, I couldn't shake the overwhelming emotions that flooded over me. I went back to Panglao, feeling like my mind was in chaos. I kept replaying everything in my head those moments when I saw her in Unitop, the brief eye contact that spoke volumes, and how I ran from her as if I were afraid of facing my past. I didn't know why I acted that way. I should have approached her, talked to her, but I was paralyzed by fear, regret, and uncertainty.

That night, as I lay in bed trying to sleep, my mind wouldn't let me forget. I was lost in the memories of our past, the good times, the bad times, and everything that had led to that moment. I couldn't help but wonder how things had gotten so complicated. It felt like I was stuck in a never-ending loop, unable to break free from the toxicity that had taken hold of my emotions.

I purchased a new SIM card. It was impulsive, perhaps even foolish, but I wanted a way to reach her without the baggage of our old conversations hanging over us. Using the new number, I texted her on WhatsApp:

"Hey, it was unexpected seeing you yesterday. You looked great. I hope you're doing well."

I waited, anxiously watching for the typing indicator. When her reply came, my heart sank:

"I think it's best if you don't text me anymore. I'm on vacation right now, and I'm happy. I don't want this to ruin my time."

Her words hit me harder than I expected. I knew I had no right to disrupt her peace, yet hearing it from her felt like a final blow. She was moving on, living her life, while I was still tethered to the past.

I stared at the message for a long time, wondering if I should reply. But what could I say? That I missed her? That I was sorry? That seeing her had reignited everything I had tried to forget? None of it would change the reality of where we stood.

In the end, I typed a simple response:

"I understand. Take care of yourself."

After sending it, I deleted her contact. It was a small step, but one I needed to take to start letting go. I couldn't keep holding on to something that wasn't mine anymore.

Still, the memory of our brief encounter lingered in my mind. It was a reminder of what once was and what could never be again. It was a painful but necessary lesson a moment that forced me to confront the truth: some chapters in life

But as much as I wanted to turn the page and leave everything behind, I realized something: I couldn't. She was still on my mind. No matter how hard I tried to push her away or pretend that I had moved on, the truth was that I hadn't. I still loved her. Despite everything that had happened, despite the pain and the heartbreak, I still had feelings for her.

In the days that followed, I tried to focus on my life, on my work because I work in 7-eleven in Modala that time because it was a vacation, on my friends, and on my own personal growth. But the constant reminder of her was there, lurking in the background of everything I did. I couldn't stop thinking about our past, the good and the bad, and the way we had both fought so hard for something that seemed impossible.

I knew that I needed to make things right with her. I couldn't let this lingering connection be defined by the mistakes I had made. I had hurt her, I had pushed her away, but deep down, I knew that I had to try again, even if it meant facing the possibility of rejection.

If she ever gave me one more chance, I promised myself I would do everything differently. I would be a better man for her, someone she could rely on and feel safe with. I learned so many lessons because of her lessons about trust, patience, and the importance of controlling my emotions. These were lessons that came too late, lessons I wished I had understood when we were still together.

But the truth was hard to ignore: it felt like she had made up her mind. She didn't want to come back, and I couldn't blame her. I had said things to her in moments of anger things I didn't mean, but that left scars nonetheless. Words are powerful, and sometimes, no matter how much you apologize, the damage remains.

To cope with everything, I buried myself in routine. I started going to the gym in Poblacion, Panglao, almost religiously. It became my sanctuary, a place where I could focus on myself and channel all the emotions I was feeling. The weights didn't judge me, and the repetitive motions of lifting and running gave me a sense of control that I hadn't felt in a long time.

After the gym, I would head to my shift at 7-Eleven in Modala, Panglao. Work kept me busy, and the constant stream of customers gave me little time to dwell on my thoughts. But during the quieter moments, her face would creep into my mind. I'd think about the times we laughed together, the way she'd roll her eyes when I tried to make her laugh after an argument, and the warmth of her voice when she told me she loved me.

Every day felt like a battle between holding on to the hope that she might come back and trying to accept that she was gone. On some nights, I'd sit outside after work, staring at the stars and wondering if she ever thought about me too. Did she miss me the way I missed her? Or had she moved on completely, leaving me behind as a memory she'd rather forget?

I thought about the times I let my emotions get the best of me. My trust issues had been a poison in our relationship, and I knew that if I ever got another chance, I would have to prove to her and to myself that I had changed. I wouldn't let jealousy dictate my actions. I would give her the space and trust she deserved.

But the harsh reality was that second chances aren't always guaranteed. Sometimes, people walk away for good, and you're left to pick up the pieces of your heart on your own. As much as I wished I could turn back time, I couldn't. All I could do was keep moving forward, even if it felt like I was carrying the weight of a thousand regrets.

The gym and work became my anchors during this time. They kept me grounded and gave me a sense of purpose when everything else felt uncertain. Slowly, I started to realize that the lessons I had learned weren't just about becoming a better partner they were about becoming a better person.

During the time I was working out regularly, life introduced me to someone unexpected with the same age. One evening at the gym, I met a Italian girl. She had this radiant presence that was hard to ignore-her bright smile, fair skin tone, and the way she carried herself with confidence. We quickly struck up a conversation, finding common ground in our passion for fitness. Over the days that followed, we talked a lot, sharing stories about our lives, our cultures, and our goals. It felt refreshing to connect with someone new, someone who seemed genuinely interested in getting to know me.

After about a week, she suggested we go out together. We decided to buy a bottle of Johnnie Walker Double Black and explore the area. She expressed interest in visiting Henann, a well-known hotel in Panglao, but admitted she wasn't familiar with the place and wanted me to accompany her. I agreed, and she insisted on paying for the hotel.

That night, we drank together in the hotel room, sharing laughs and stories as the alcohol loosened our inhibitions. As the night wore on, the mood shifted, and we found ourselves drawn to each other in a way that felt both unexpected and inevitable. One thing led to another, and we ended up having sex. It was intense, passionate, and exhausting a moment of connection that left us both breath'

The next morning, we woke up naked, the sunlight streaming through the windows of the hotel room. The reality of what had happened hit me as I looked over at her. She was stunning, even in the raw vulnerability of the morning light. We talked briefly, shared a quiet breakfast, and went our separate ways for the day.

Two days later, she returned to Italy. We said our goodbyes, knowing our connection was fleeting and that our lives were headed in different directions. There was no talk of staying in touch or continuing whatever it was that had started between us. It was a moment in time, a brief escape from the complexity of my emotions and my life.

Yet, as I went back to my routine- working at 7-Eleven, going to the gym, and trying to move forward- my thoughts kept drifting back to my ex. The encounter with the Italian girl had been a distraction, a way to momentarily forget the lingering ache of heartbreak. But it didn't work. If anything, it made me realize how much my ex still occupied my mind and my heart.

Every time I thought about the unexpected moment when I ran into my ex, it brought back a flood of memories-both good and bad. I wondered if she ever thought about me the way I thought about her. Did she miss me? Or was she truly happy, as she had said, without me in her life?

The Italian girl had been a beautiful chapter, but she wasn't the one who held the deepest part of my soul. That part still belonged to my ex, no matter how hard I tried to move on. It was a harsh reminder that you can't escape your feelings, no matter how far you run or how many new experiences you try to create. Some emotions linger, refusing to be drowned out by the noise of life.

Chapter 8: Rising Above the Past

As time passed and I reflected on my journey, my life took a dramatic turn for the better. I resigned from my job at 7-Eleven, driven by a renewed sense of purpose. My focus shifted back to school, as I realized the importance of completing my education and finishing my Grade 12. It wasn't just about finishing school; it was about setting myself up for success, laying the foundation for the future I wanted to build.

While juggling school, I managed to write my first book, From Ground Zero to Fortune. The process took eight months, but the effort was worth it. I poured my heart and soul into it, sharing the lessons I had learned about perseverance, self-improvement, and the importance of never giving up. The book not only became a reflection of my journey but also an international success. Sales grew steadily, and I was amazed by the global reach it gained.

The success of the book gave me the confidence to pursue bigger dreams. I founded Nexgrow Marketing Agency, a business that quickly began to thrive. I started with just one client, but within a short time, I had 19 clients, helping their businesses grow through digital marketing strategies. The idea of starting something from scratch and watching it evolve into a successful venture was incredibly fulfilling.

I was determined not to make the same financial mistakes I had in the past. I carefully managed my money, ensuring that every cent I earned went back into my business. I didn't spend a single peso on liabilities or personal expenses; instead, I focused on making my money work for me. The lessons I had learned from my past relationships and mistakes were invaluable. They taught me the importance of discipline, patience, and the need to delay gratification.

Writing my second book, The Algorithmic Uprising, was a different experience. It only took a month to complete, as I used some paid tools to help streamline the process. I invested my personal money in the project, rather than using business funds, but I knew it was an investment in my future. I had learned not to rely on emotional impulses, but on calculated decisions that aligned with my long-term goals.

One of the biggest lessons I had learned from my past relationships, particularly my love experiences, was the importance of focusing on my career and personal growth before getting involved in marriage or serious relationships. I had seen how distractions in love could take away from my focus on building my future. I made a decision that, no matter how much I desired companionship, I would wait until I had achieved the success I envisioned before considering marriage. I set a goal to marry at 40, after establishing myself as a multi-millionaire, with several significant businesses under my belt.

I wanted to ensure that when I did marry, I would be financially stable, with a legacy to share. My focus was no longer on love or relationships that could potentially derail me from my goals. Instead, my energy was directed toward becoming a wealthy, successful person someone who would have a profound impact on others and who could build something that would last for generations.

Through all the ups and downs, I learned that the journey to success is never linear. There will be setbacks, moments of doubt, and challenges that test your resolve. But with persistence, discipline, and a clear vision of what you want, anything is possible. And as I moved forward, I felt more confident than ever in my path, knowing that I was building something truly meaningful.

Don't miss out!

Visit the website below and you can sign up to receive emails whenever Ivan Lloyd Roquero publishes a new book. There's no charge and no obligation.

https://books2read.com/r/B-A-BHITC-YICKF

BOOKS 2 READ

Connecting independent readers to independent writers.

Also by Ivan Lloyd Roquero

Algorithmic Uprising
From Ground Zero to Fortune
The Man Who Loved Again

About the Author

I am a driven young entrepreneur, author, and fitness enthusiast from Bohol, Philippines . I am driven by a passion for knowledge and innovation, aiming to provide readers with practical insights and strategies for success. Through my works, I blends research, experience, and vision to inspire growth and resilience in a rapidly evolving world.

www.ingramcontent.com/pod-product-compliance
Lightning Source LLC
LaVergne TN
LVHW040905150826
845672LV00007B/1901

* 9 7 9 8 2 3 0 0 7 8 9 5 1 *